BASS RECORDED VERSIONS

AVENGED SEV...
NIGHTMARE

2   NIGHTMARE

11   WELCOME TO THE FAMILY

18   DANGER LINE

27   BURIED ALIVE

37   NATURAL BORN KILLER

46   SO FAR AWAY

54   GOD HATES US

60   VICTIM

74   TONIGHT THE WORLD DIES

81   FICTION

86   SAVE ME

102   Bass Notation Legend

Bass transcriptions by Martin Shellard

ISBN 978-1-61774-121-0

HAL•LEONARD®
CORPORATION

7777 W. BLUEMOUND RD. P.O. BOX 13819 MILWAUKEE, WI 53213

In Australia Contact:
Hal Leonard Australia Pty. Ltd.
4 Lentara Court
Cheltenham, Victoria, 3192 Australia
Email: ausadmin@halleonard.com.au

Visit Hal Leonard Online at
www.halleonard.com

Nightmare

Words and Music by Matthew Sanders, Jonathan Seward, James Sullivan, Brian Haner, Jr. and Zachary Baker

♩ = 128

Now ___ your night - mare comes ___ to life. _____

Verse

1. Dragged you down be - low,   down to the Dev - il's   show ___
2. Can't wake up in sweat   'cause it ain't o - ver   yet. ___

Bass Fig. 1

to be his guest for - ev - er. ___   Peace of mind is less than nev - er! ___
Still danc - ing with your de - mons.   Vic - tim of your own cre - a - tion! ___

End Bass Fig. 1

Bass: w/ Bass Fig. 1

Hate to twist your mind,   but God ain't on your side. ___
Be - yond the will to fight,   where all that's wrong is right, ___

3

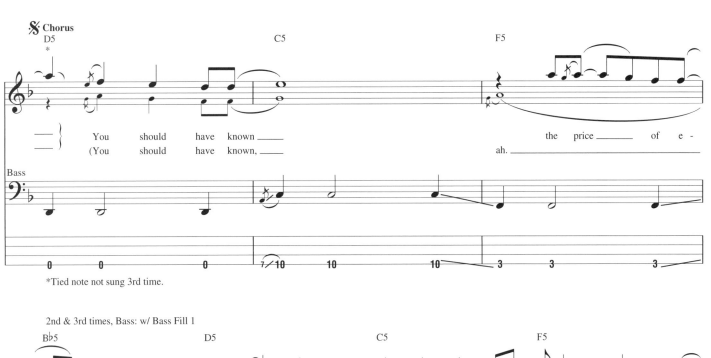

*Tied note not sung 3rd time.

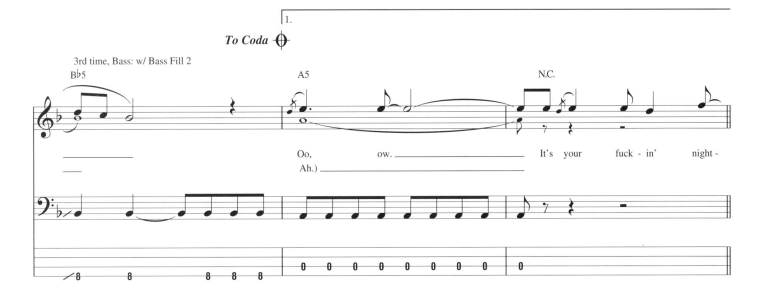

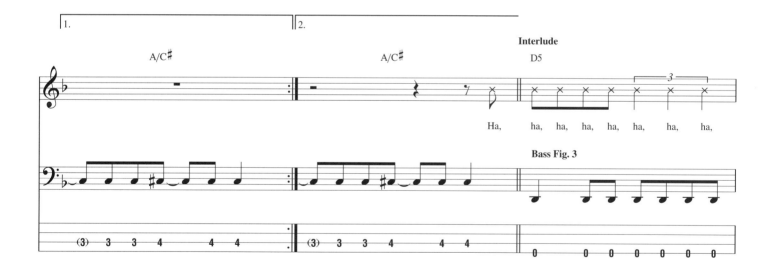

And I know they may _ seem real,... ...these sig-nals of love. _

But our life's made up _ of choic - es... ...some with-out ap - peal.)

End half-time feel

They took for grant - ed your soul, _____ and it's ours now _ to steal _

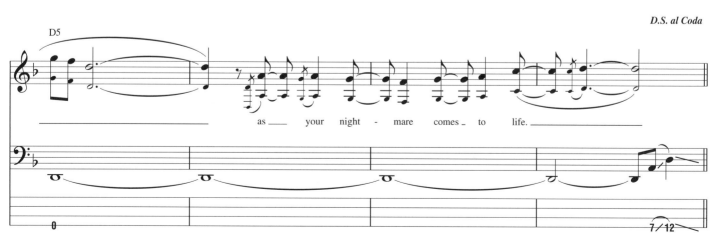

D.S. al Coda

as _ your night - mare comes _ to life. _

Coda

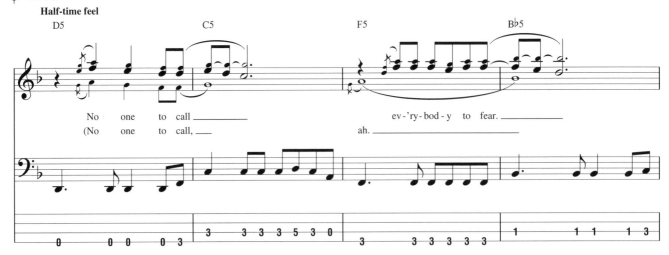

No one to call _____ ev-'ry-bod-y to fear. _____
(No one to call, _____ ah. _____

Your trag-ic fate _____ is look-ing so _____ clear, _____ yeah. _____
Your trag-ic fate _____ is look-ing so _____ clear, _____

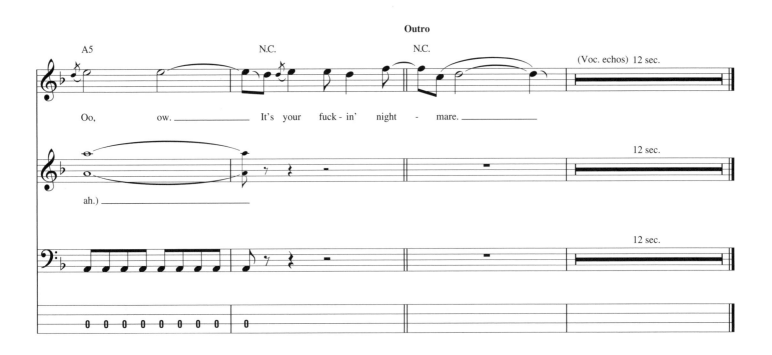

Oo, ow. _____ It's your fuck-in' night - mare. _____
ah.) _____

Welcome to the Family

Words and Music by Matthew Sanders, Jonathan Seward, James Sullivan, Brian Haner, Jr. and Zachary Baker

11

Psy-chot-ic, rab-id de-men-tia, I won't be fine.

Guitar Solo
Double-time feel

End double-time feel

Bridge

I _____ see _____ you're a king who's _____ been de-throned, _____
(I _____ see, stand a-lone. _____)

*Chord symbols reflect overall harmony.

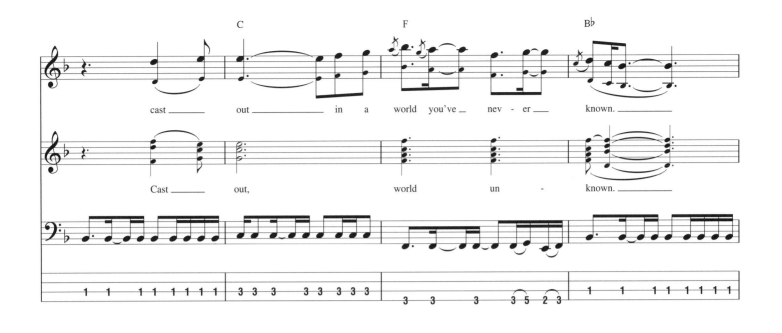

cast _____ out _____ in a world you've _____ nev - er _____ known. _____

Cast _____ out, _____ world un - known. _____

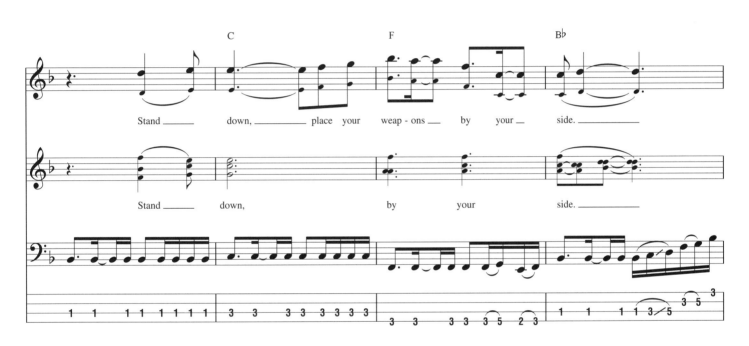

Stand _____ down, _____ place your weap - ons _____ by your _____ side. _____

Stand _____ down, _____ by your _____ side. _____

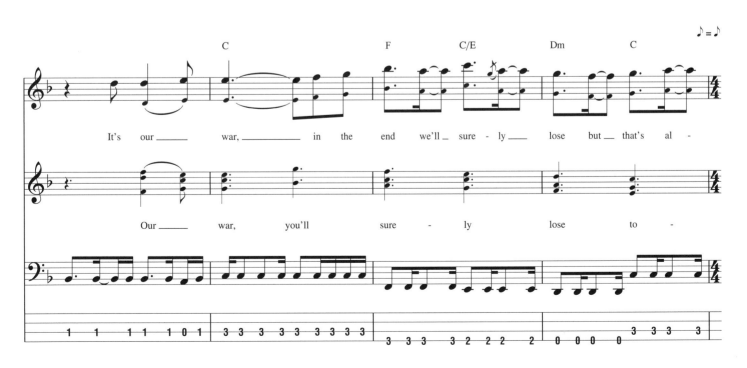

It's our _____ war, _____ in the end we'll sure - ly _____ lose but _____ that's al -

Our _____ war, you'll sure - ly lose to -

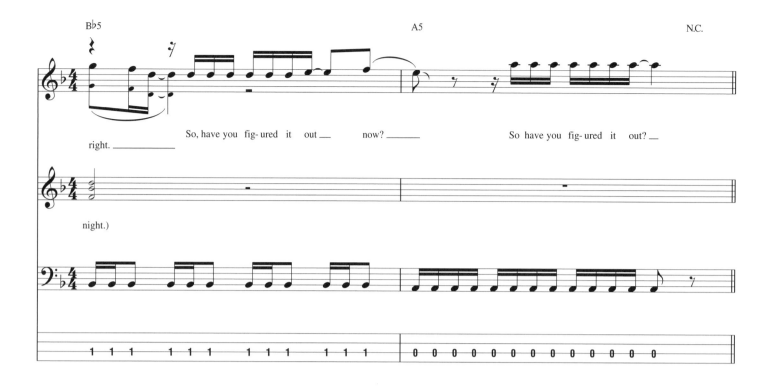

So, have you fig-ured it out ___ now? _____ So have you fig-ured it out? ___

right. _____

night.)

Chorus

And in a way ___ it seems ___ there's ___ no one ___ to call when ___ our ___

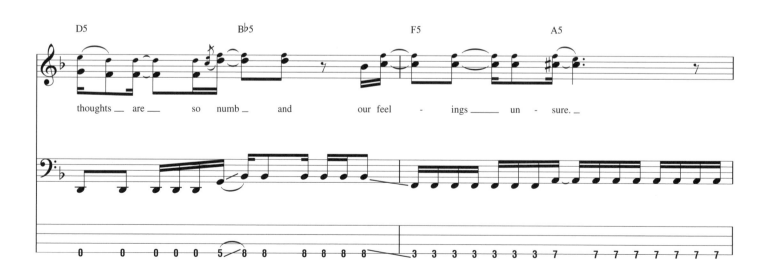

thoughts ___ are ___ so numb ___ and our feel - ings _____ un - sure. ___

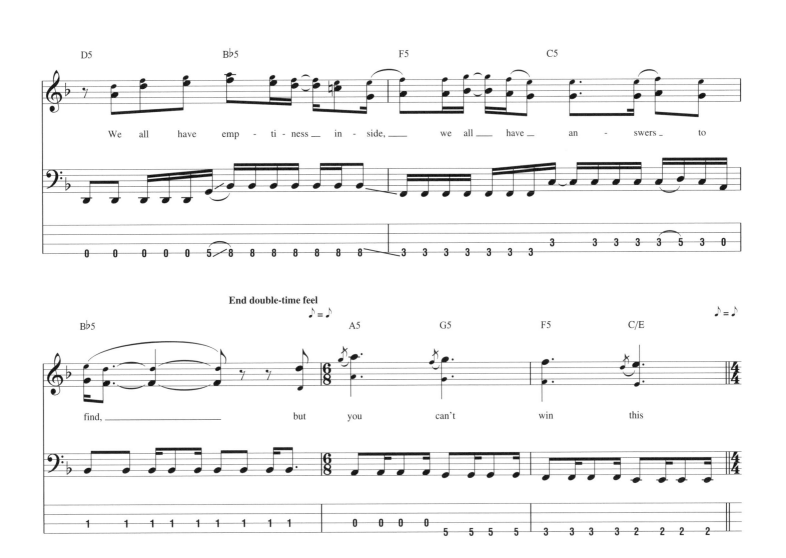

We all have emp-ti-ness in-side, ___ we all ___ have an - swers ___ to

End double-time feel

find, _____ but you can't win this

Deep in - side, where noth-ing's fine, I lost my mind.
fight.

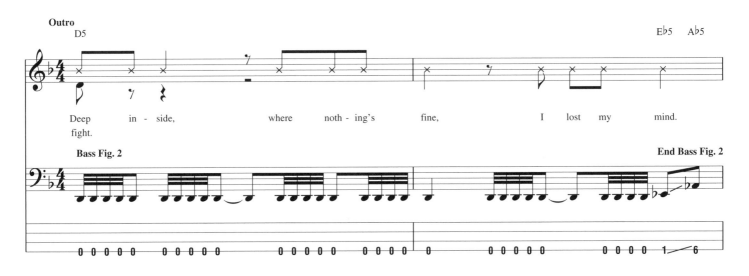

Outro

Bass Fig. 2

End Bass Fig. 2

Bass: w/ Bass Fig. 2 (3 times)

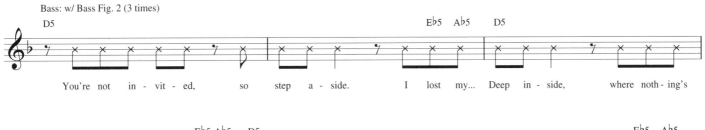

You're not in - vit - ed, so step a - side. I lost my... Deep in - side, where noth - ing's

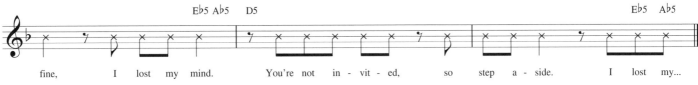

fine, I lost my mind. You're not in - vit - ed, so step a - side. I lost my...

Danger Line

Words and Music by Matthew Sanders, Jonathan Seward, James Sullivan, Brian Haner, Jr. and Zachary Baker

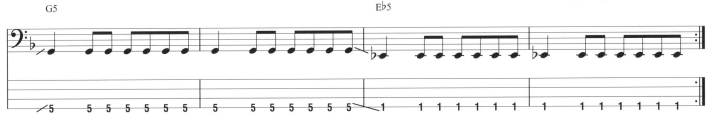

𝄋 Verse

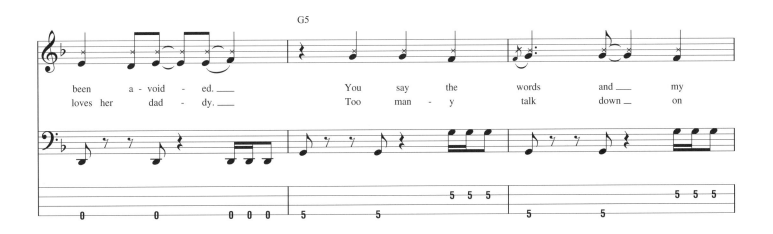

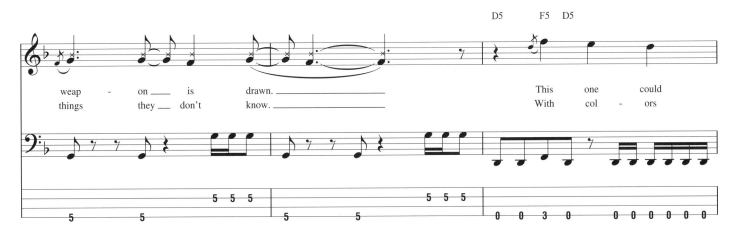

Verse lyrics:

1. My six-teen locked and load-ed, ___ all fear has been a-void-ed. ___ You say the words and ___ my weap-on ___ is drawn. ___ This one could

2. I do this for my fam-'ly, ___ my daugh-ter loves her dad-dy. ___ Too man-y words talk down ___ on things they ___ don't know. ___ With col-ors

be my last _____ time, _____ some peo - ple call it war - crime. _____
nev - er fad - ed, _____ reck - less and un - a - bat - ed. _____

I may be star - ing down _____ a le - thal sight... _____
They may take me but nev - er take us all, _____

Bass tacet
N.C.

to die. _____
I'll crawl. _____

Chorus
Double-time feel

Noth - ing shocks you like a bul - let _____ hole. _____

Bass Fig. 1

Bass

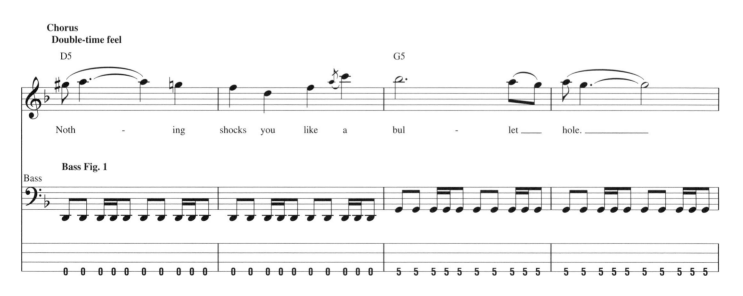

Coda

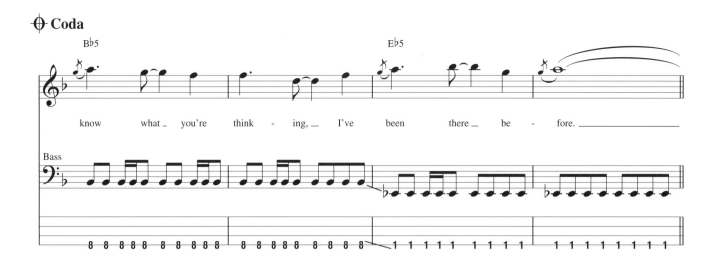

know what _ you're think - ing, _ I've been there _ be - fore. _____

Bridge

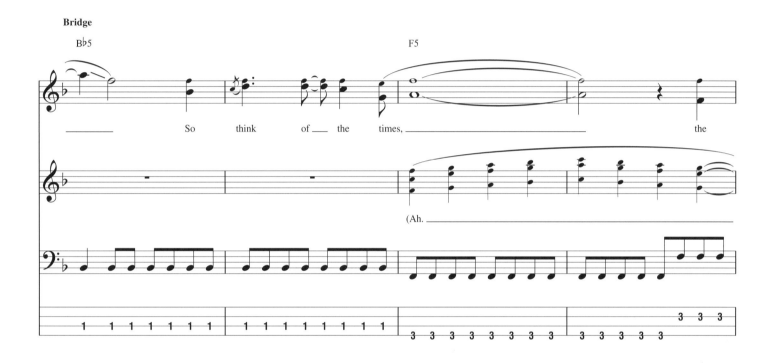

_____ So think of _ the times, _____ the

(Ah.

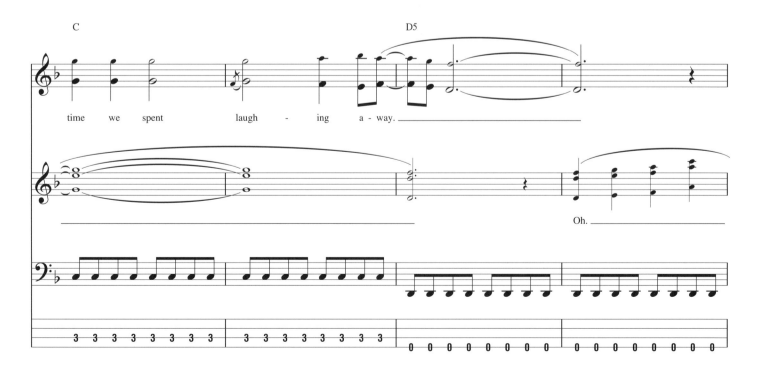

time we spent laugh - ing a - way. _____

Oh. _____

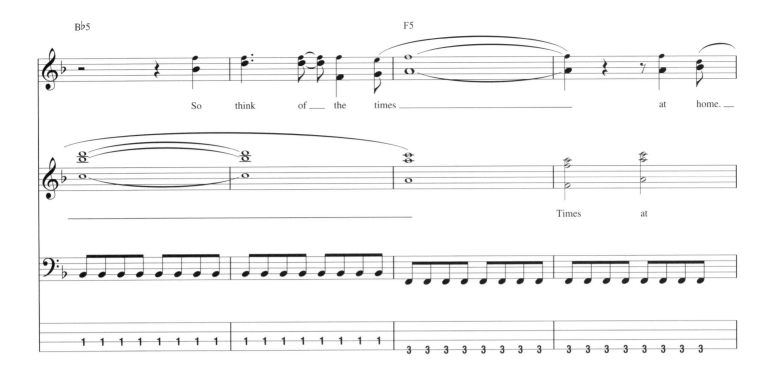

So think of the times _____ at home. _____

Times at

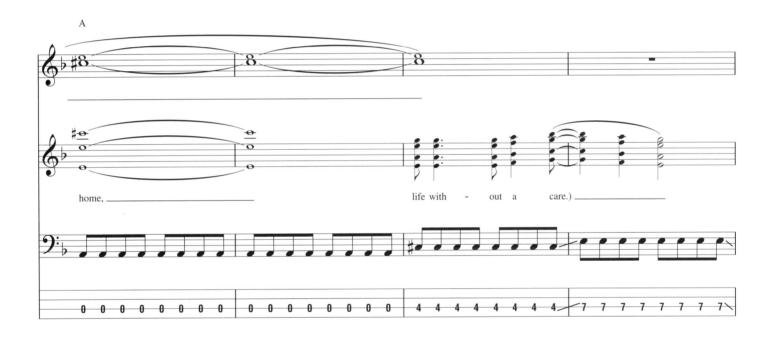

home, _____

life with - out a care.) _____

Now I find ___ my - self _____ in my ___ own blood, ___

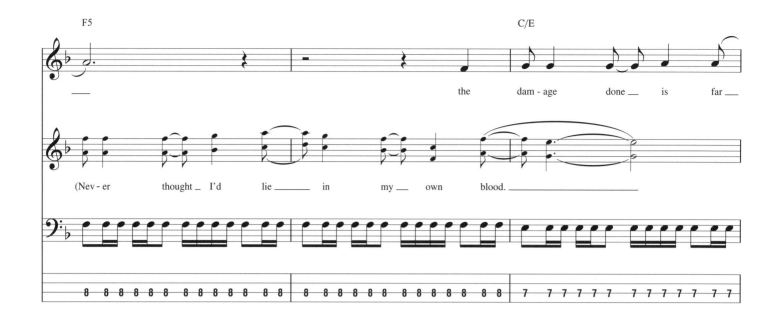

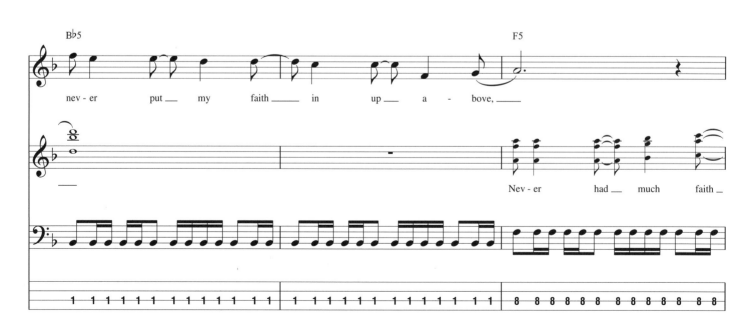

A

but now _____ I'm
_____ in up a- bove. I'm

8 8 8 8 8 8 8 8 8 8 8 8   0 0 0 0 0 0 0 0 0 0 0 0   0 0 0 0 0 0 0 0 0 0 0 0

End double-time feel

hop - ing _____ some - one's there. _____ I

(hop - ing _____ some - one's there.) _____

4 4 4 4 4 4 4 4 4 4 4 4   7 7 7 7 7 7 7 7 7

Bridge
Slower ♩ = 91
Bass tacet

B♭   F   B♭/F   C/E

nev - er meant _ to leave _ this world _ a - lone. _____ I nev - er meant _ to hurt _ the ones _ who care. _

Dm   B♭   F

_____ And all this time _ I thought _ we'd just _ grow old. _____ You know, _

A   Asus4   A+   A   B♭

_ no one said it's fair. _ Tell my ba - by girl that it's al -

F   B♭/F   C/E   Dm

right, I've sung my last song _____ to - day. _ Re - mind the

Lord   to leave His light ____ on   for me... _____   I'm free. __

Guitar Solo

Bass

Outro

Bass tacet

Whistled: -

Begin fade   *Fade out*

(Snare drum & piano)

8

Whistled: -

Buried Alive

Words and Music by Matthew Sanders, Jonathan Seward, James Sullivan, Brian Haner, Jr. and Zachary Baker

Drop D tuning:
(low to high) D-A-D-G

Intro
Moderately fast ♩ = 138

*Chord symbols reflect implied harmony.

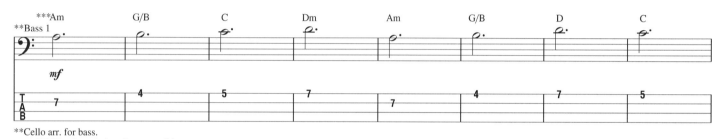

**Cello arr. for bass.
***Chord symbols reflect overall harmony.

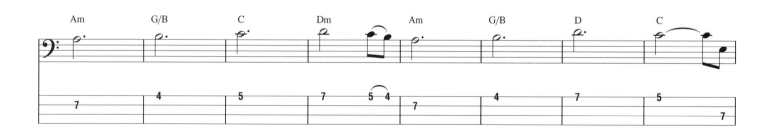

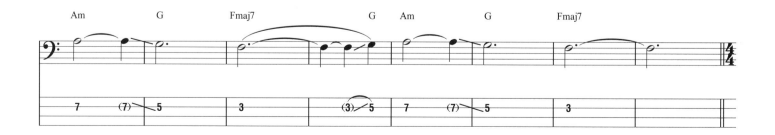

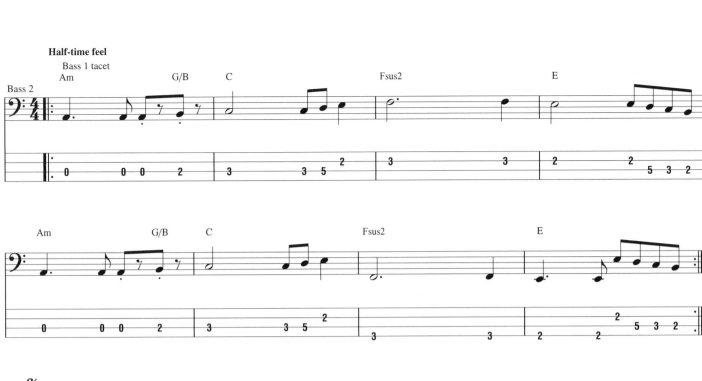

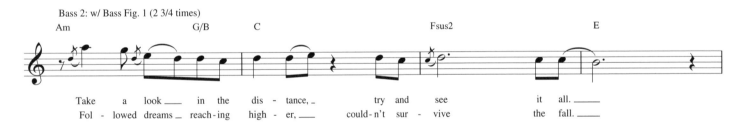

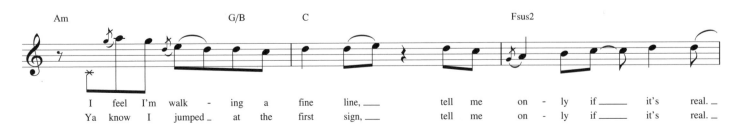

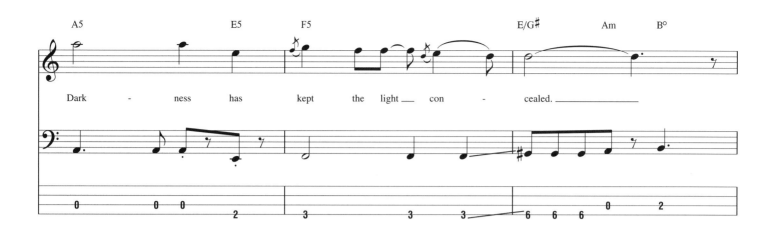

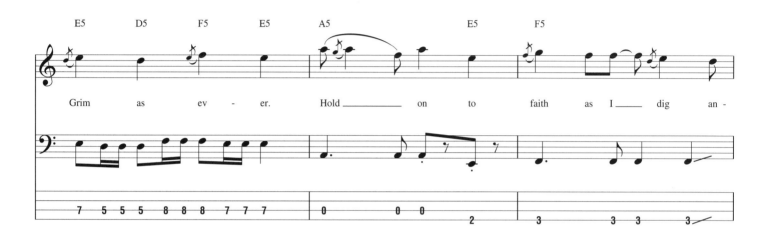

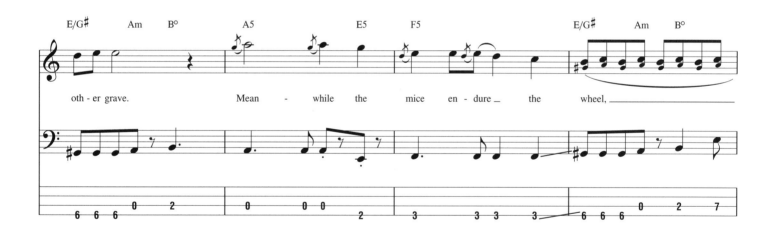

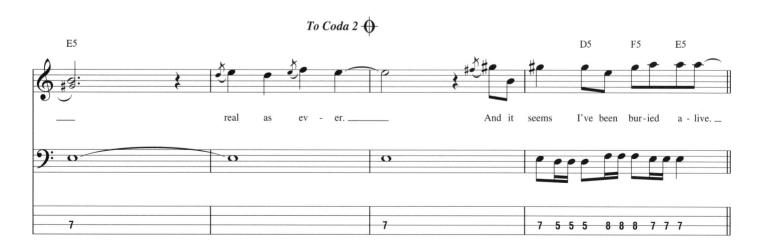

Interlude

D.S. al Coda 1

⊕ Coda 1

Pre-Chorus

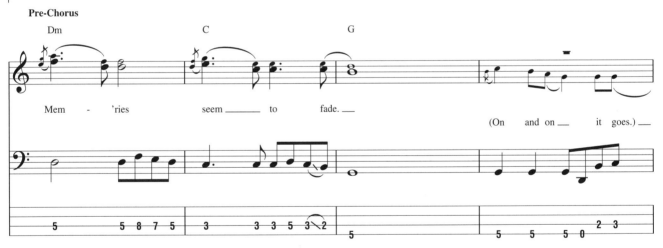

Mem - 'ries seem ____ to fade. ____

(On and on ____ it goes.) ____

D.S.S. al Coda 2

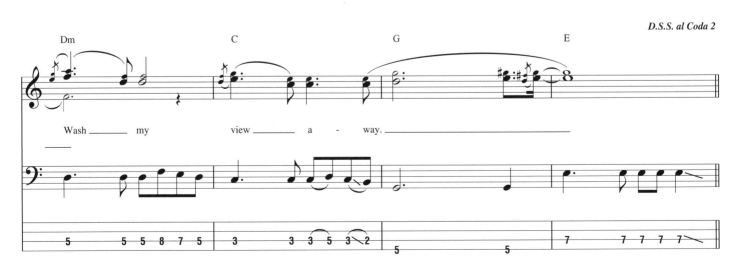

Wash ____ my view ____ a - way. ____

⊕ Coda 2

And I'm chained like ___ a slave, _____ trapped in ___ the dark.

End half-time feel

Slammed all ___ the locks, death calls ___ my name and it seems I've been bur - ied a - live. ___

Interlude

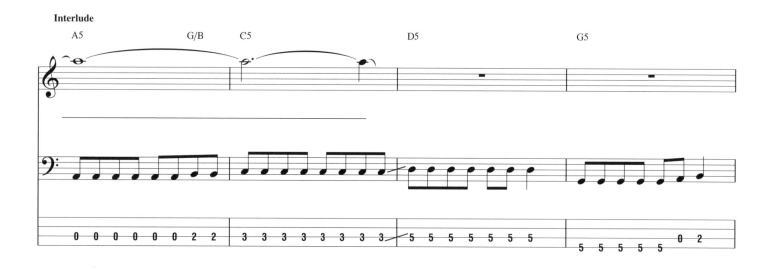

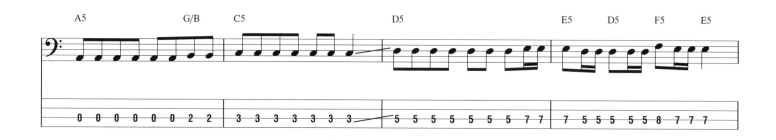

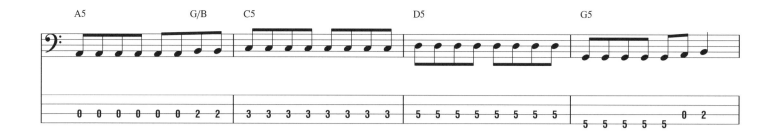

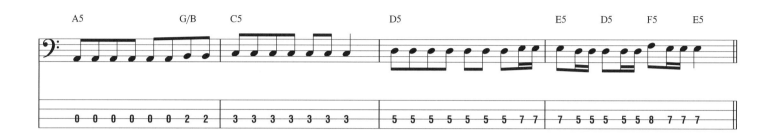

Guitar Solo

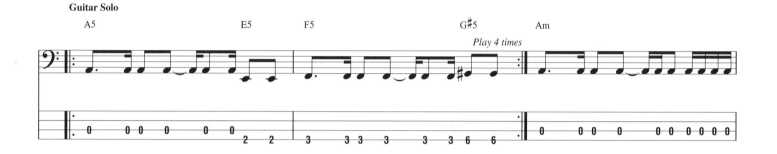

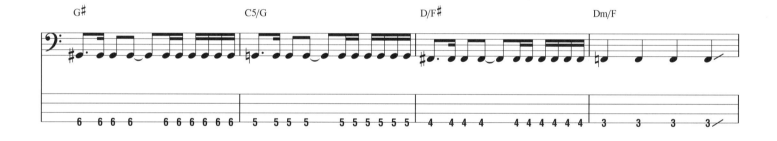

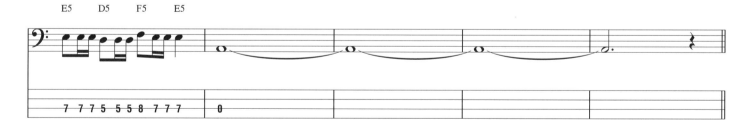

Interlude

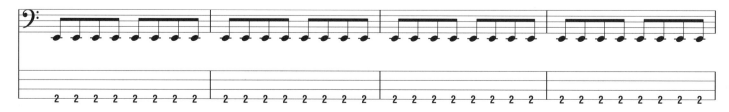

Guitar Solo

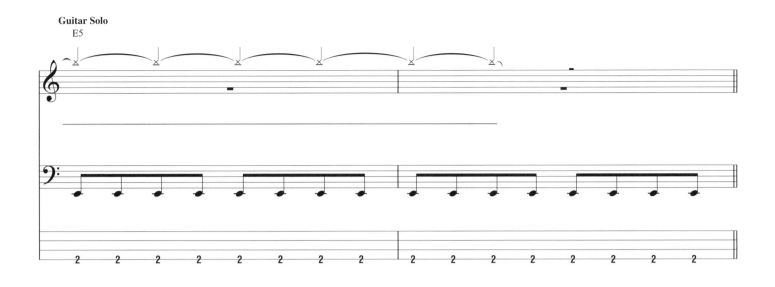

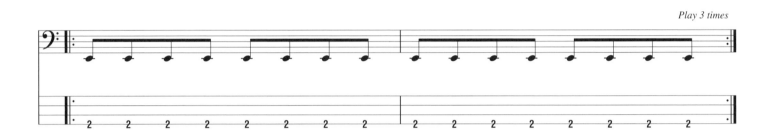

Play 3 times

Outro

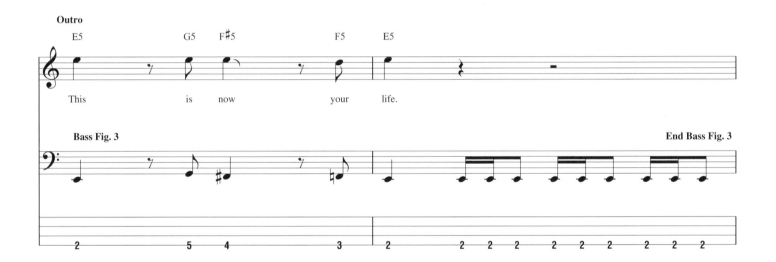

This is now your life.

Bass Fig. 3 ... **End Bass Fig. 3**

Bass 2: w/ Bass Fig. 3 (3 times)

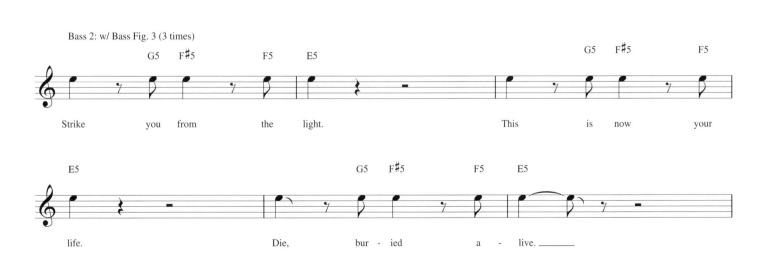

Strike you from the light. This is now your

life. Die, bur-ied a-live. _____

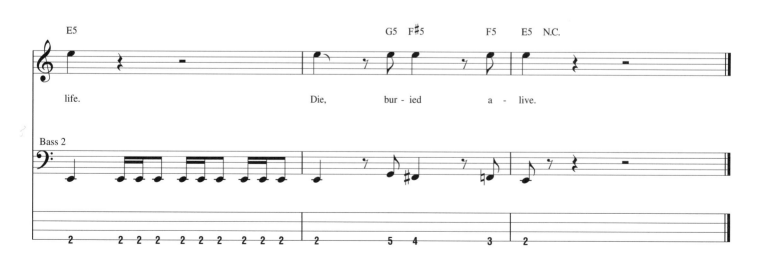

Natural Born Killer

Words and Music by Matthew Sanders, Jonathan Seward, James Sullivan, Brian Haner, Jr. and Zachary Baker

Drop D tuning:
(low to high) D-A-D-G

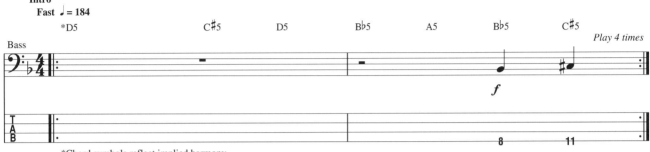

*Chord symbols reflect implied harmony.

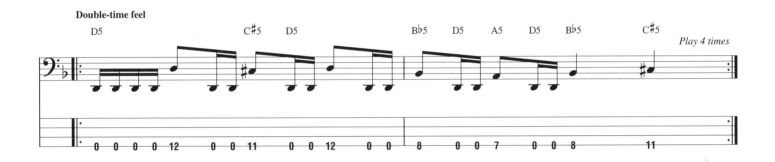

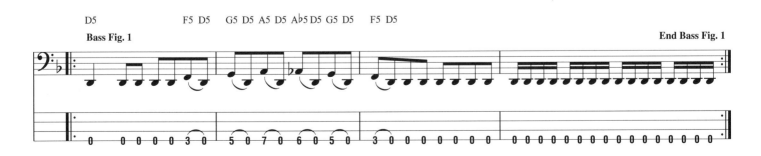

So this is ___ the world you ___ left ___ be - hind? ___
So this is ___ the hate I've ___ been ___ born to? ___

This is ___ the guilt that ___ con - sumes you? So
Full are ___ the tales of ___ the un - true.

Chorus
Half-time feel

die ___ a - lone. ___ This is ___ the

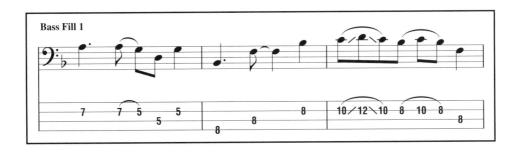

Bass Fill 1

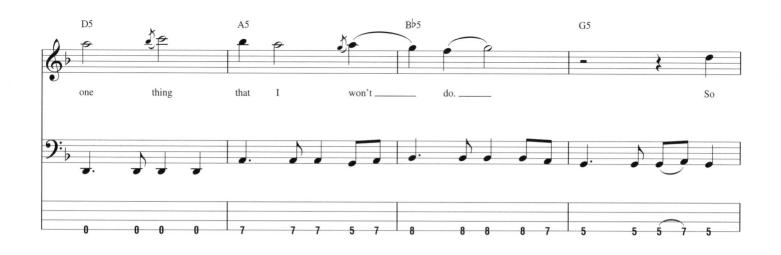

one   thing   that   I   won't _____ do. _____   So

say _____ your   prayers, _____   'cause   I   ain't

To Coda ⊕

leav -   ing   here   with - out _____ you. _____

End half-time feel

40

Interlude

2nd time, D.S. al Coda

Coda

Guitar Solo

Bridge

Bass: w/ Bass Fig. 3 (3 1/2 times)

And I'm wait - in', wait - in' for _____ the days to slow - ly _____ pass _____ me by. _____ (And all the prom - is - es I'll No hes - i - tat - ing, you pull the trig - find.) _____ - ger, now your sto - ry's _____ left _____ be - hind. _____

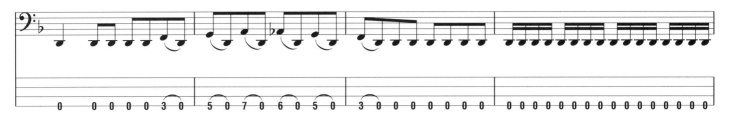

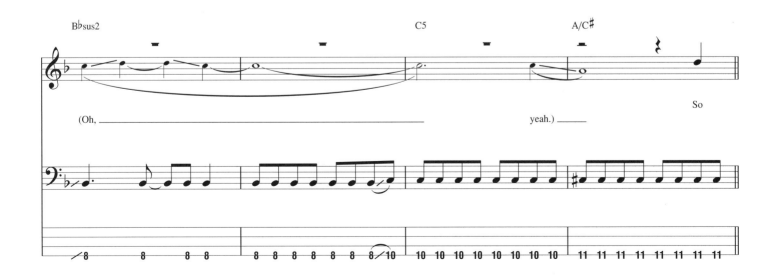

So Far Away

Words and Music by Matthew Sanders, Jonathan Seward, James Sullivan, Brian Haner, Jr. and Zachary Baker

Verse
Moderately slow ♩ = 76

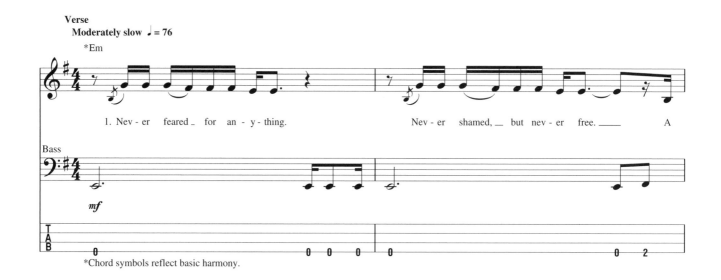

1. Nev - er feared for an - y - thing. Nev - er shamed, but nev - er free. A

*Chord symbols reflect basic harmony.

light that healed a bro - ken heart with all that it could. Lived a life so end - less - ly.

Saw be - yond what oth - ers see. I tried to heal your bro - ken heart with all that I could.

Chorus

D   Em

Will you stay, _____ will you stay a - way _ for - ev - er? How do I live with - out the

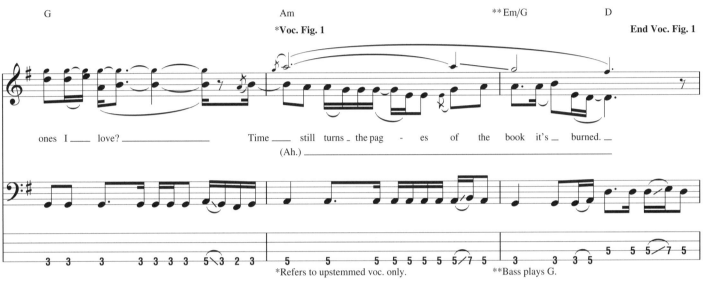

G   Am   **Em/G   D

*Voc. Fig. 1   End Voc. Fig. 1

ones I _____ love? _____ Time _____ still turns _ the pag - es of the book it's _ burned. _
           (Ah.) _____

*Refers to upstemmed voc. only.   **Bass plays G.

Em   G   Bkgd. Voc.: w/ Voc. Fig. 1
             Am

Place and time _____ al - ways on my mind. _____ I have _ so much _ to say _ but you're so

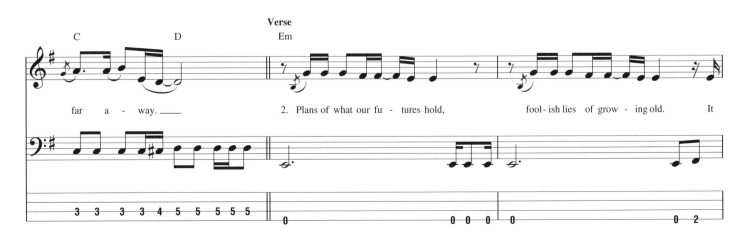

C   D   Verse
           Em

far a - way. _____ 2. Plans of what our fu - tures hold, foolish lies of grow - ing old. It

47

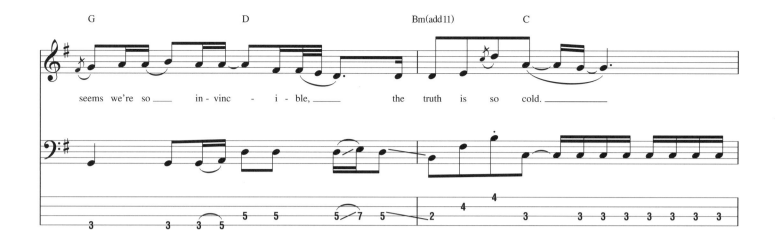

seems we're so __ in - vinc - i - ble, __ the truth is so cold. __

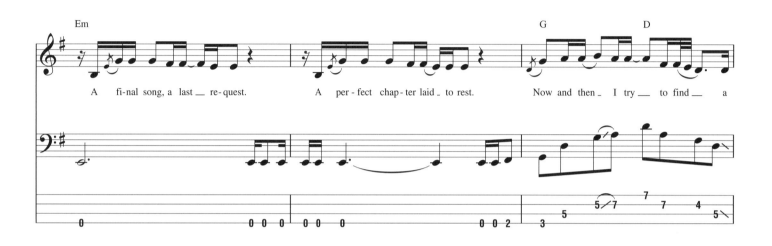

A fi - nal song, a last __ re - quest. A per - fect chap - ter laid __ to rest. Now and then __ I try __ to find __ a

place in my mind __ where you can stay, __ you can stay a - wake __ for - ev - er.

Chorus

Bkgd. Voc.: w/ Voc. Fig. 1

How do I live __ with - out the ones I love? Time __ still turns the pag - es of the

soon as I'm done   I'll   be on   my way _____ to live _____ e - ter - nal - ly. _____
(On   my   way.)

Guitar Solo

***Em/G**

*Bass plays G.

Chorus

Bkgd. Voc.: w/ Voc. Fig. 1

How do I live _____ with - out the ones I _____ love? _____   Time _____ still turns _ the pag _ - es of the

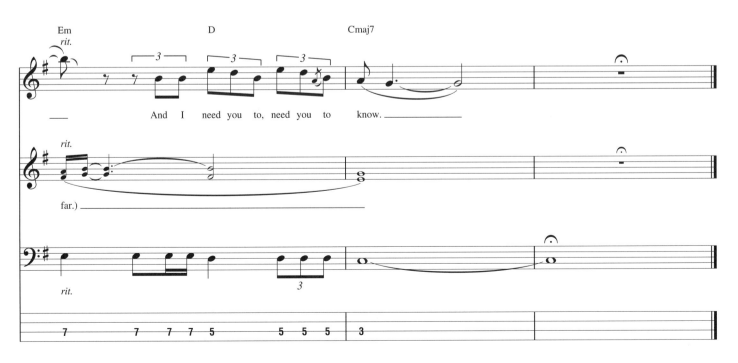

God Hates Us

Words and Music by Matthew Sanders, Jonathan Seward, James Sullivan, Brian Haner, Jr. and Zachary Baker

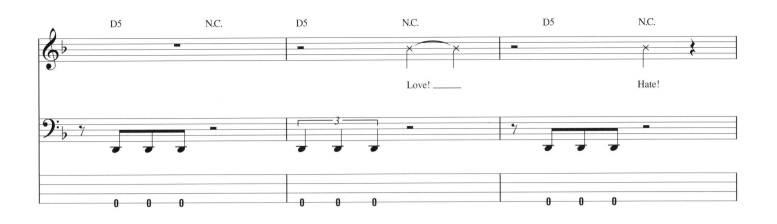

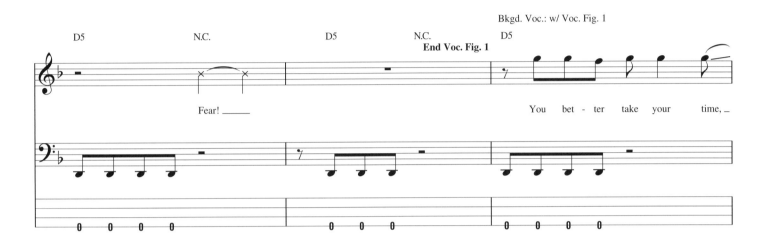

Victim

Words and Music by Matthew Sanders, Jonathan Seward, James Sullivan, Brian Haner, Jr. and Zachary Baker

Drop D tuning, down 1 step:
(low to high) C-G-C-F

Intro
Moderately ♩ = 130

*Dm
(Guitar)

16

*Chord symbols reflect implied harmony.

Half-time feel

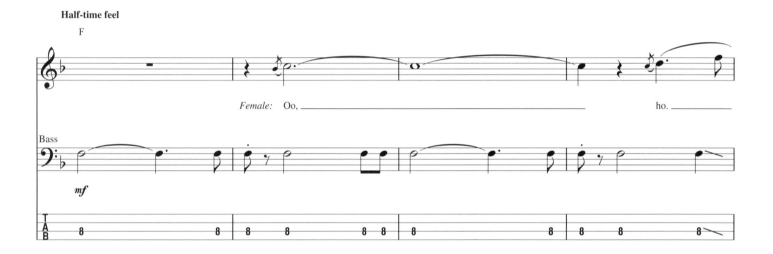

Female: Oo, _____ ho. _____

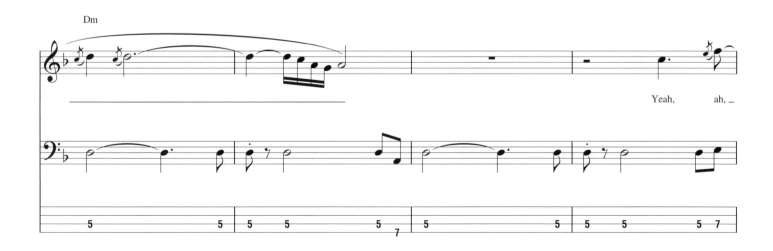

_____ Yeah, ah, ___

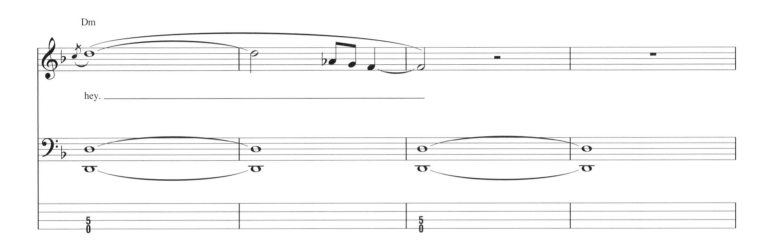

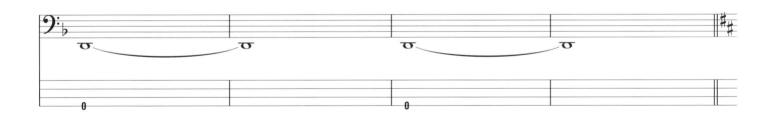

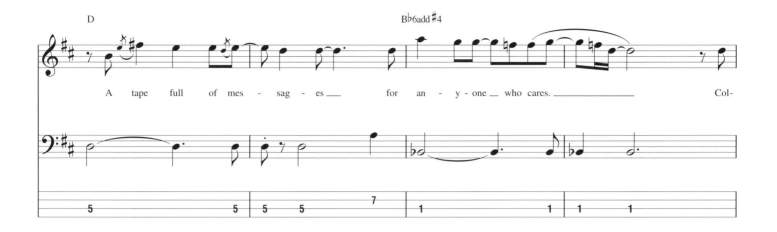

A tape full of mes - sag - es ___ for an - y - one ___ who cares. ___ Col-

lage of bro - ken words ___ and sto - ries full ___ of tears. ___ Re-

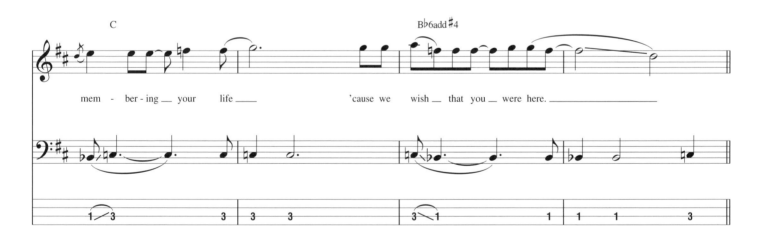

mem - ber - ing ___ your life ___ 'cause we wish ___ that you ___ were here. ___

Verse

2. Noth - ing is hard - er ___ than to wake up all ___ a - lone, ___

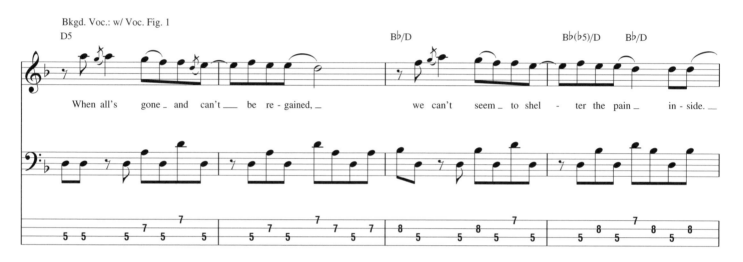

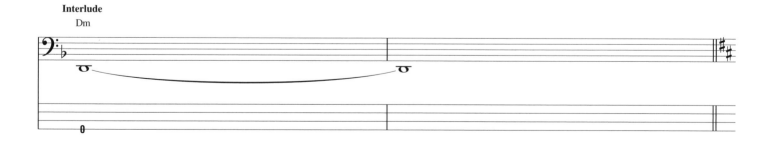

Interlude

Dm

Verse

3. Some days you'll find ___ me ___ in a place I like ___ to go, ___

ask ques - tions to ___ my - self ___ 'bout the things I'll nev - er know. ___

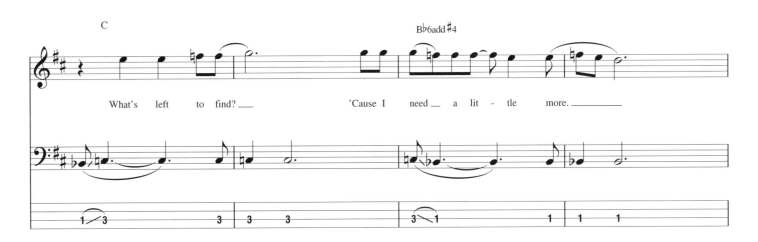

What's left to find? ___ 'Cause I need ___ a lit - tle more. ___

I need a lit - tle time. ___ Can we e - ven up ___ the score? ___

Bkgd. Voc.: w/ Voc. Fig. 1 (2 times)

And some say __ this can't __ be __ real, __ and I've lost __ my pow - er to feel __ to - night. __

__ We're all __ just vic - tims of __ a crime. ___

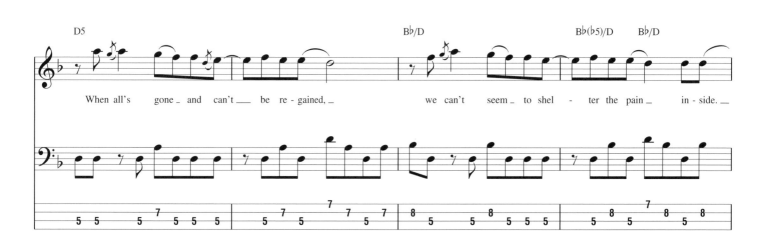

When all's gone __ and can't __ be re - gained, __ we can't seem __ to shel - ter the pain __ in - side. __

End half-time feel

__ Oo, ___ we're all __ just vic - tims of __ a crime. ___

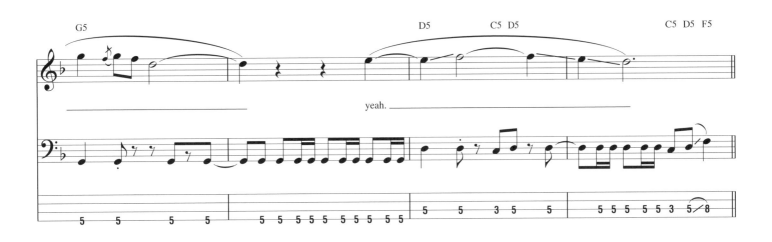

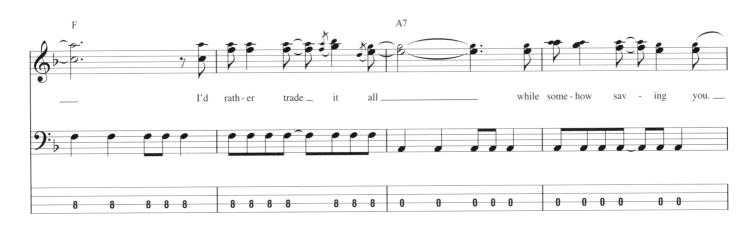

It must have been __ the sea - son __ that threw us out __ of line. __

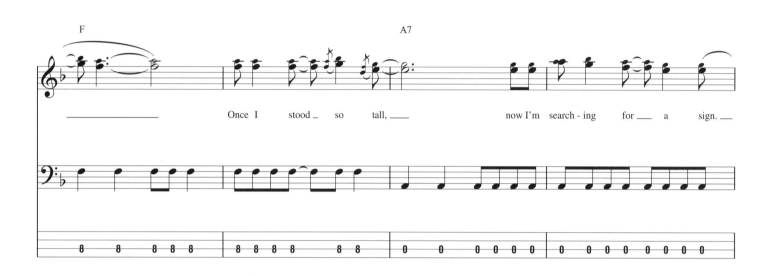

Once I stood __ so tall, __ now I'm search - ing for __ a sign. __

Half-time feel

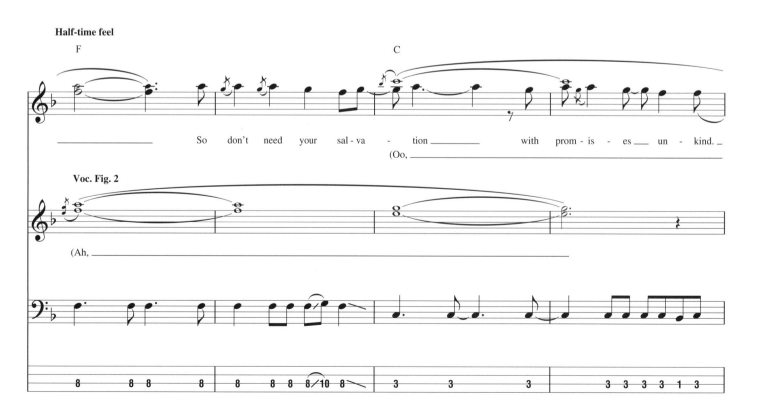

So don't need your sal - va - tion __ with prom - is - es __ un - kind. __
(Oo, __

Voc. Fig. 2

(Ah, __

And all the spec - u - la - tion, _____ save it for an - oth - er time. ___
oo. _____

ah.) _____

End Voc. Fig. 2

Bkgd. Voc.: w/ Voc. Fig. 2

'Cause we all need __ a rea - son, _____ a rea - son just __ to stay. __
Oo, _____

End half-time feel

Well, some just can't __ be both - ered _____ to stick a - round an - oth - er day. __
oo.) _____

Interlude

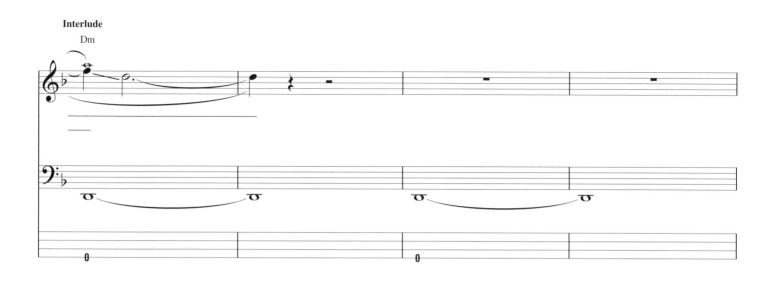

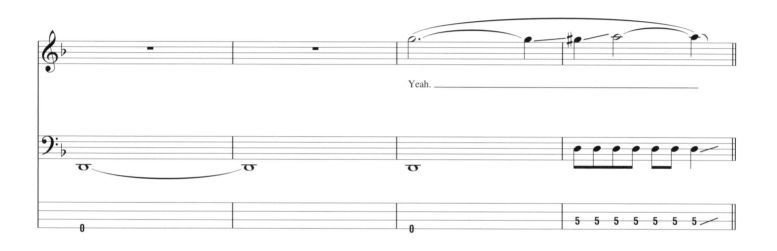

Yeah.

Guitar Solo

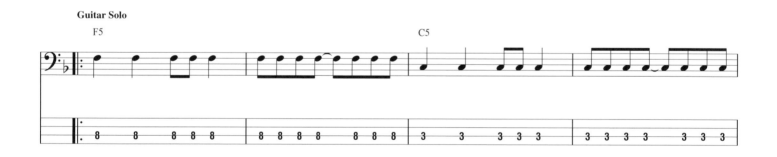

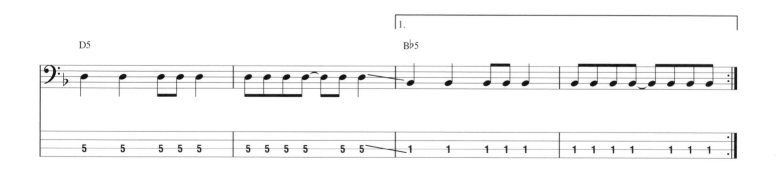

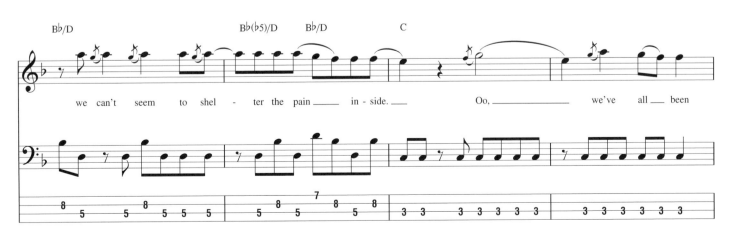

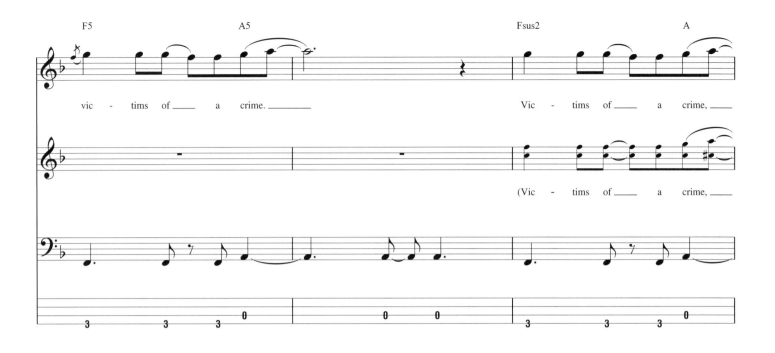

End half-time feel

Interlude

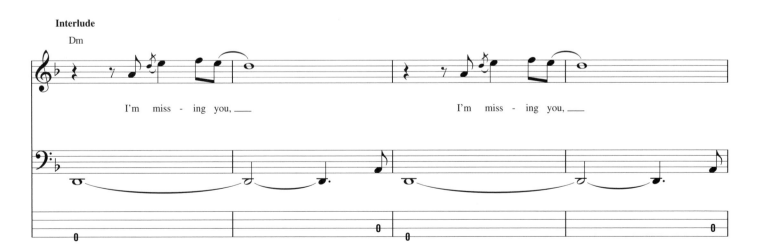

I'm miss - ing you, ____ I'm miss - ing you. ____

Outro
Bass tacet
Fsus2

Female: Ah, _____ yeah, _____

Dm   Dsus2   Dm   Dsus4   Dm

oh. _____

Fsus2   F

Ah, _____ ha, ____ ah. _____

Dm   Dsus2   Dm   Dsus4

Ha, _____ yeah, ____ hey. _____

F   Fsus4   F   Fadd9   F

Hey, ____ hey, ____ yeah, _____

Dm   C/D   Dm

hoo, ____ hoo, ____ ho. _____

Fadd9   Fsus²   Fadd9   C   Dm

Ho, _____ ho. _____

Tonight the World Dies

Words and Music by Matthew Sanders, Jonathan Seward, James Sullivan, Brian Haner, Jr. and Zachary Baker

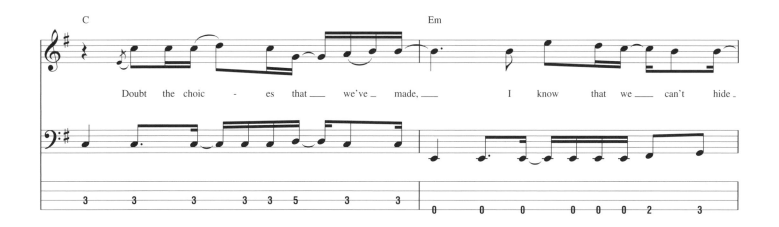

Doubt the choic - es that ___ we've ___ made, ___ I know that we ___ can't hide ___

___ our shame. ___ It's on - ly in ___ dis - guise. ___

Interlude

Bkgd. Voc.: w/ Voc. Fig. 1 (2 times)

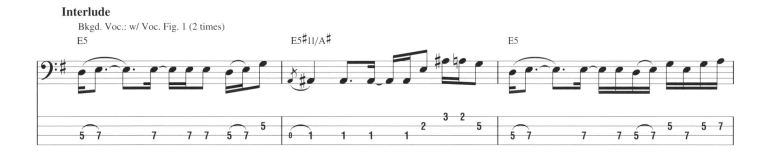

Verse

2. Drown - ing in ___ our own de - bris. ___

Fool our thoughts _ as though _ we're _ free. _ Close our eyes _ so we _ can see _

_ the depth of all _ we mean _ to be. _ If on - ly in my _ eyes. _

Chorus

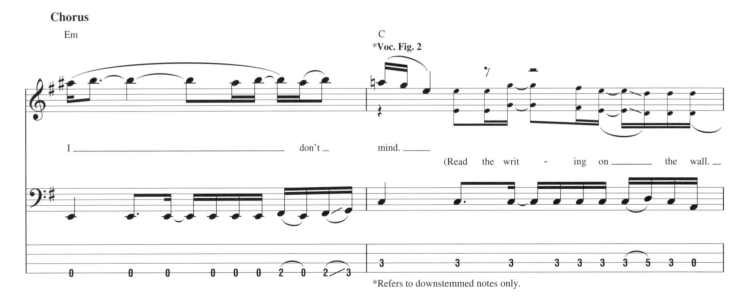

I _ don't _ mind. _ (Read the writ - ing on _ the wall. _

*Refers to downstemmed notes only.

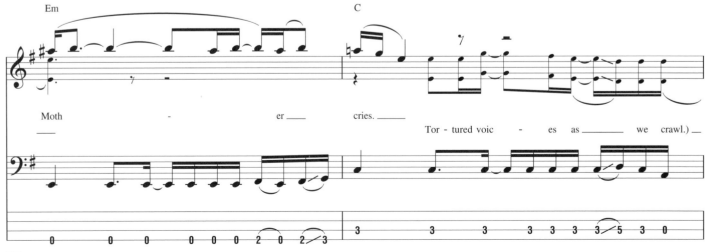

Moth - er _ cries. _ Tor - tured voic - es as _ we crawl.) _

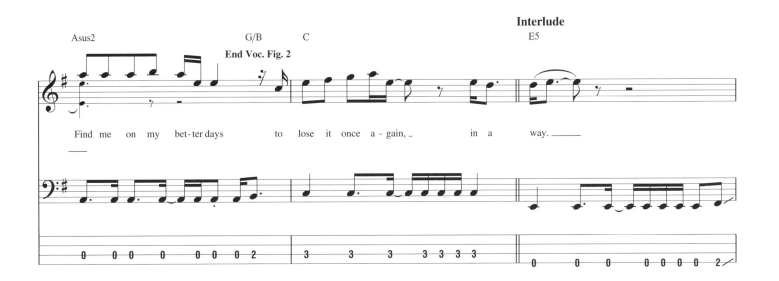

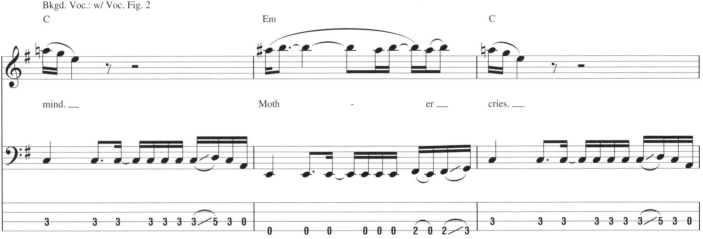

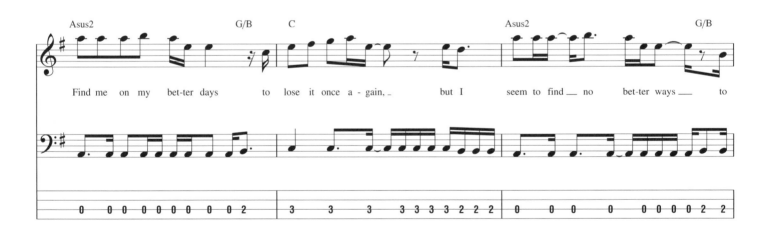

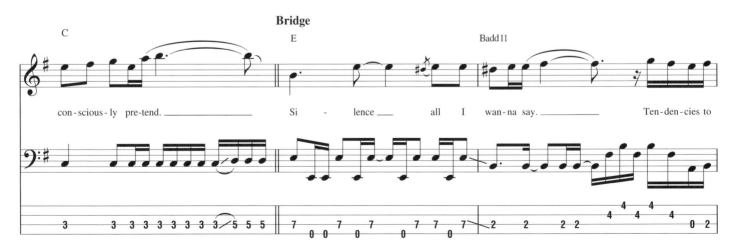

run a - way, I run a - way _____ with you to - night. _____

Laun - der _____ all my sins a - way. _____ And just like that mis-

takes are made, you know. _____ To - night the __ world _____

Chorus

Bkgd. Voc.: w/ Voc. Fig. 2

dies. _____ Don't _ mind. _____

Outro

Bkgd. Voc.: w/ Voc. Fig. 1 (3 times)

Fiction

Words and Music by Matthew Sanders, Jonathan Seward, James Sullivan, Brian Haner, Jr. and Zachary Baker

Drop D tuning, down 1 step:
(low to high) C-G-C-F

*Piano arr. for bass.

**Chord symbols reflect basic harmony.

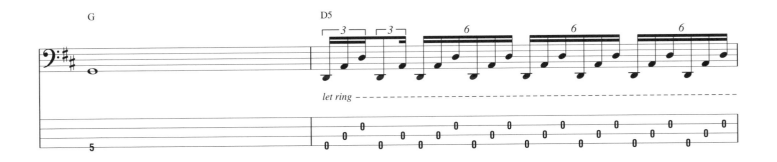

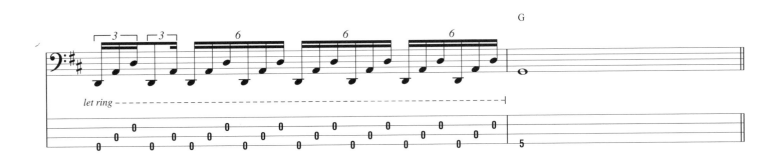

Verse

1. Now I think I un-der-stand ___ how this world can o-ver-come ___ a man. ___

Like a friend we saw it through. ___ In the end, I gave my life ___ for you. ___

Interlude

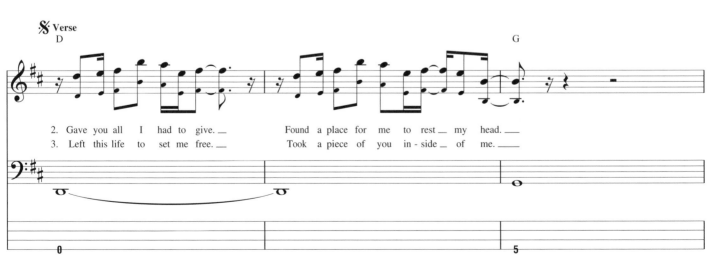

let ring

Verse

2. Gave you all I had to give. ___ Found a place for me to rest ___ my head. ___
3. Left this life to set me free. ___ Took a piece of you in-side ___ of me. ___

While I may be hard to find, _____ heard there's peace just on the oth - er side. _____
All this hurt can fi - nal - ly fade. _____ Prom - ise me you'll nev - er feel _____ a - fraid. _____

Chorus

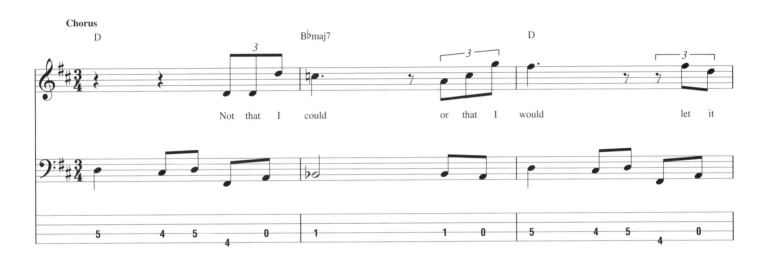

Not that I could or that I would let it

To Coda ⊕

burn _____ un - der my _____ skin, _____ let it burn. _____

Interlude

D.S. al Coda

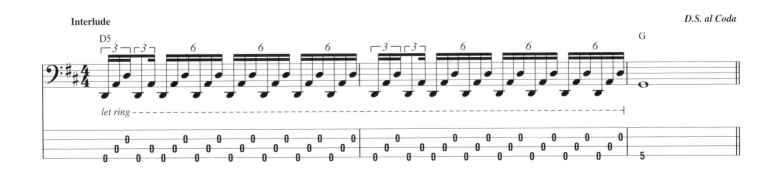

let ring -

Coda

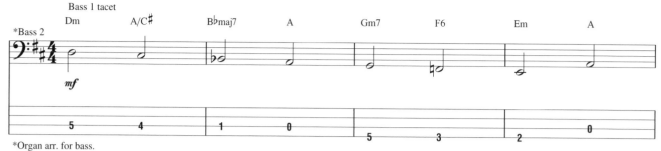

*Organ arr. for bass.

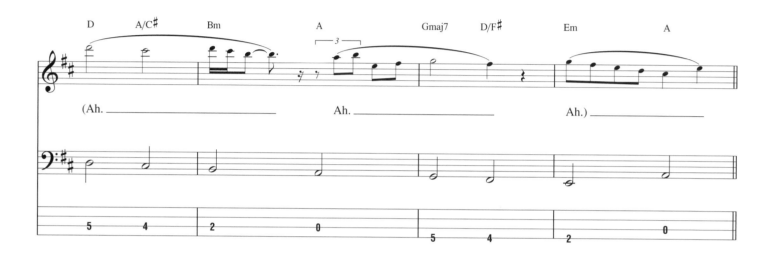

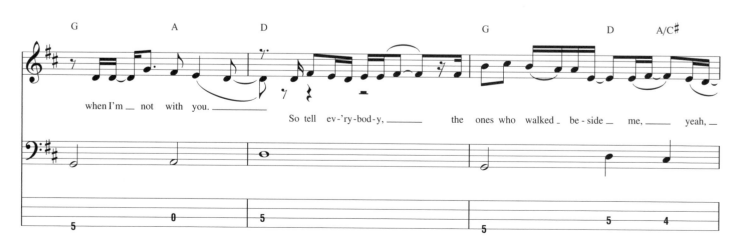

Save Me

Words and Music by Matthew Sanders, Jonathan Seward, James Sullivan, Brian Haner, Jr. and Zachary Baker

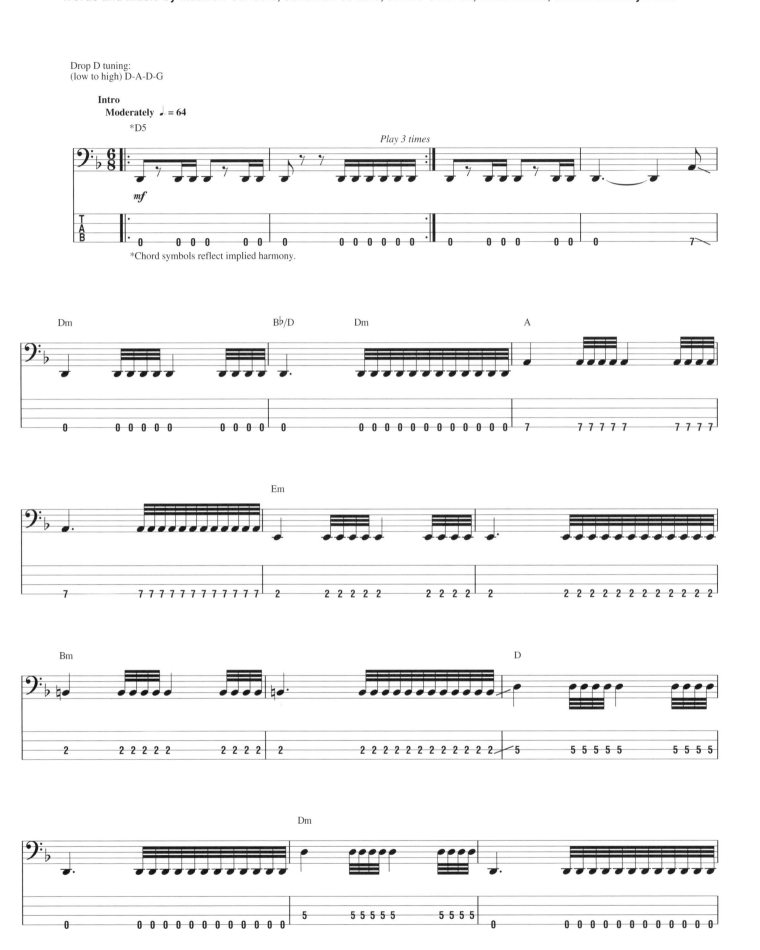

*Chord symbols reflect implied harmony.

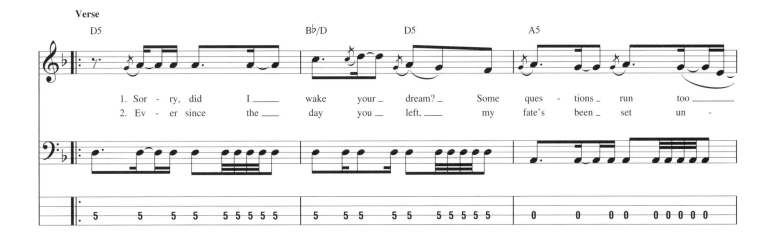

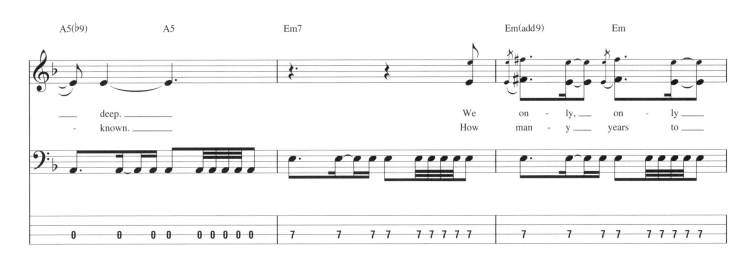

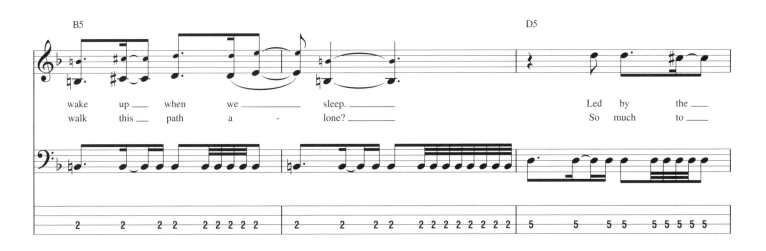

𝄉 **Chorus**

*Refers to downstemmed notes only.

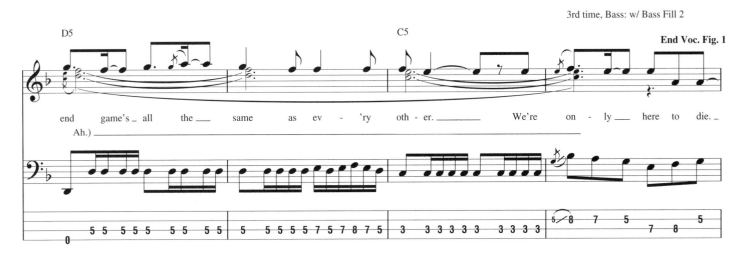

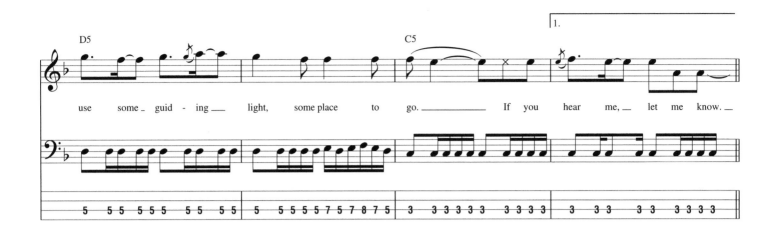

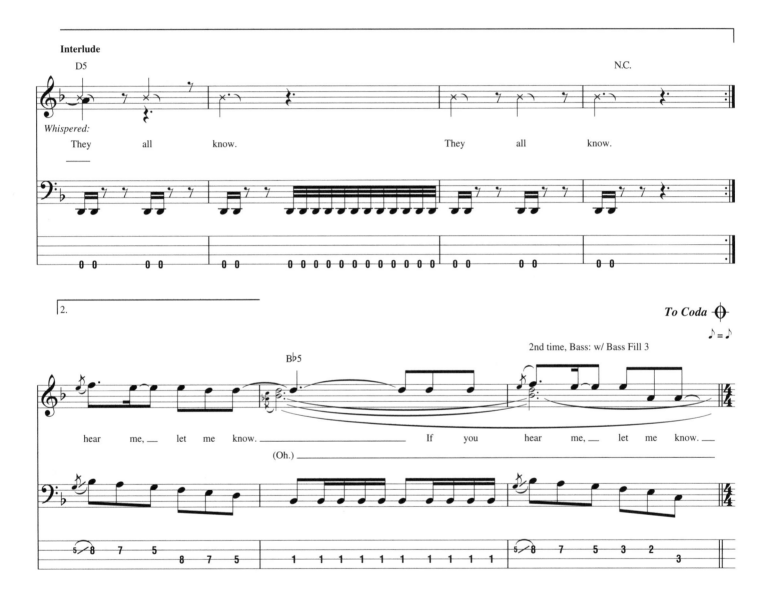

Interlude

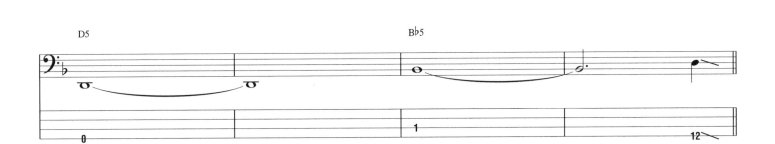

Guitar Solo
Quadruple-time feel

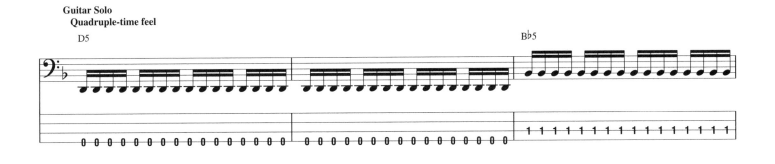

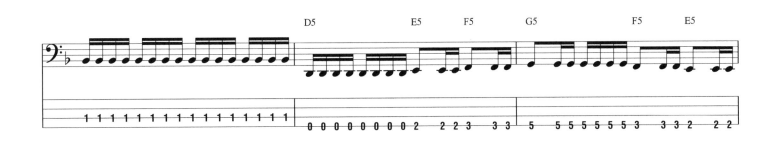

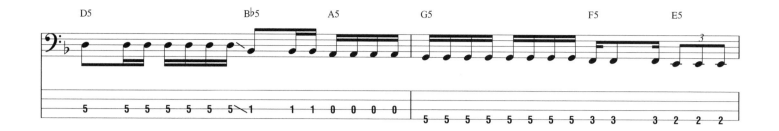

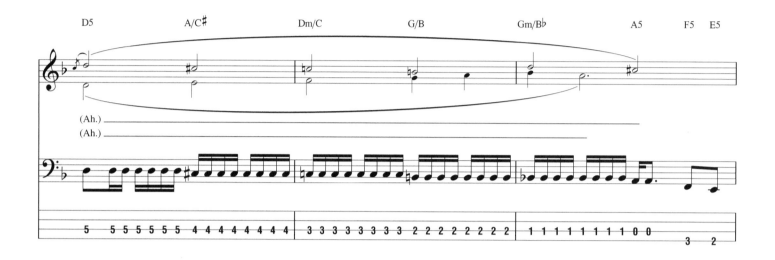

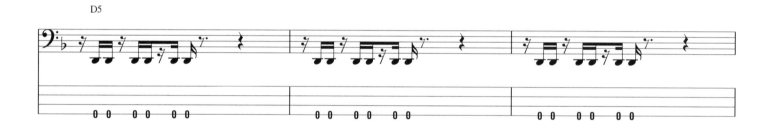

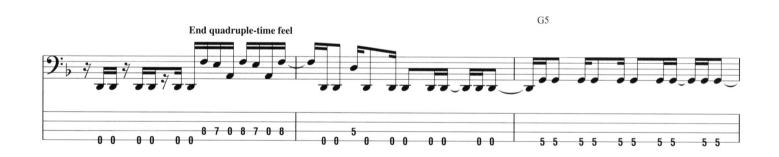

Interlude

Bridge

guise. _____ They say that all beau-ty must die, I say it ___ just moves _

on.

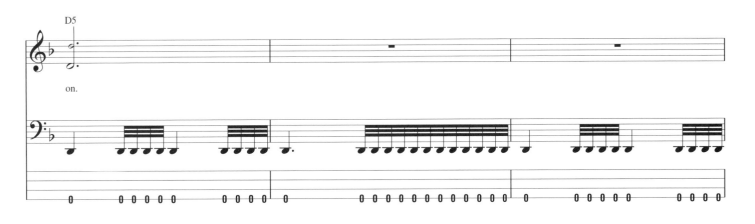

If you'd on - ly ___ o - pen your mind, then

some - day ___ you will ___ find _____ in - san - i - ty left us be -

hind   and   walked   right _ through   the _ door.   I   can _ see   the _

pic - tures _ clear _ as   yes - ter - day, _____   pic - tures _ all   my _

D.S. al Coda
(take 2nd ending)

I   can _ hear   the _ voic - es _ beg - ging   you   to   stay, _ but   know   you're _ not   a -
own.

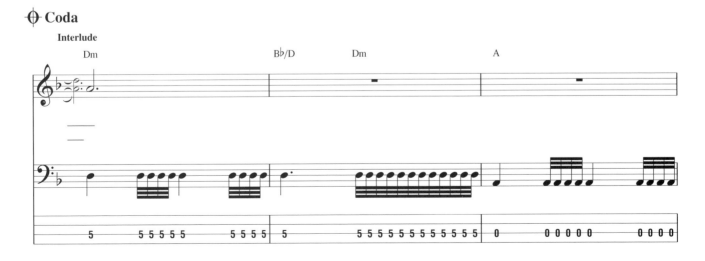

⊕ Coda

Interlude

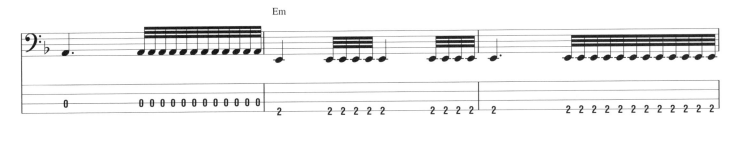

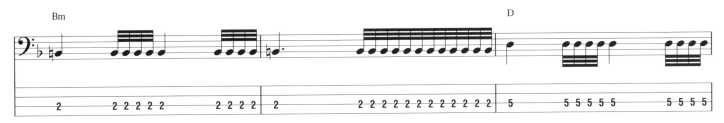

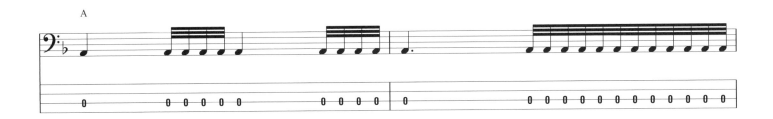

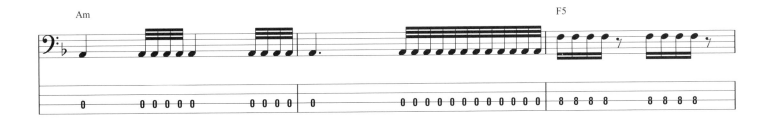

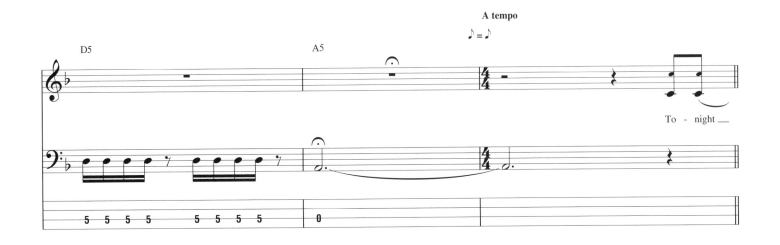

Outro

BASS NOTATION LEGEND

Bass music can be notated two different ways: on a *musical staff*, and in *tablature*.

THE MUSICAL STAFF shows pitches and rhythms and is divided by bar lines into measures. Pitches are named after the first seven letters of the alphabet.

TABLATURE graphically represents the bass fingerboard. Each horizontal line represents a string, and each number represents a fret.

Notes:

Strings: high — low

3rd string, open

2nd string, 2nd fret

1st & 2nd strings open, played together

HAMMER-ON: Strike the first (lower) note with one finger, then sound the higher note (on the same string) with another finger by fretting it without picking.

PULL-OFF: Place both fingers on the notes to be sounded. Strike the first note and without picking, pull the finger off to sound the second (lower) note.

LEGATO SLIDE: Strike the first note and then slide the same fret-hand finger up or down to the second note. The second note is not struck.

SHIFT SLIDE: Same as legato slide, except the second note is struck.

TRILL: Very rapidly alternate between the notes indicated by continuously hammering on and pulling off.

TREMOLO PICKING: The note is picked as rapidly and continuously as possible.

VIBRATO: The string is vibrated by rapidly bending and releasing the note with the fretting hand.

SHAKE: Using one finger, rapidly alternate between two notes on one string by sliding either a half-step above or below.

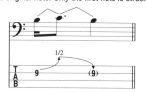

NATURAL HARMONIC: Strike the note while the fret hand lightly touches the string directly over the fret indicated.

MUFFLED STRINGS: A percussive sound is produced by laying the fret hand across the string(s) without depressing them and striking them with the pick hand.

BEND: Strike the note and bend up the interval shown.

BEND AND RELEASE: Strike the note and bend up as indicated, then release back to the original note. Only the first note is struck.

RIGHT-HAND TAP: Hammer ("tap") the fret indicated with the "pick-hand" index or middle finger and pull off to the note fretted by the fret hand.

LEFT-HAND TAP: Hammer ("tap") the fret indicated with the "fret-hand" index or middle finger.

SLAP: Strike ("slap") string with right-hand thumb.

POP: Snap ("pop") string with right-hand index or middle finger.

Additional Musical Definitions

> (accent) • Accentuate note (play it louder).

^ (accent) • Accentuate note with great intensity.

. (staccato) • Play the note short.

⊓ • Downstroke

∨ • Upstroke

D.S. al Coda • Go back to the sign (𝄋), then play until the measure marked "*To Coda*," then skip to the section labelled "*Coda*."

D.C. al Fine • Go back to the beginning of the song and play until the measure marked "*Fine*" (end).

Bass Fig. • Label used to recall a recurring pattern.

Fill • Label used to identify a brief melodic figure which is to be inserted into the arrangement.

tacet • Instrument is silent (drops out).

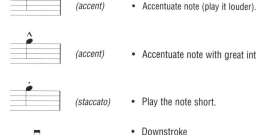

• Repeat measures between signs.

• When a repeated section has different endings, play the first ending only the first time and the second ending only the second time.

NOTE: Tablature numbers in parentheses mean:
1. The note is being sustained over a system (note in standard notation is tied), or
2. The note is sustained, but a new articulation (such as a hammer-on, pull-off, slide or vibrato) begins.

Hal•Leonard BASS PLAY-ALONG™

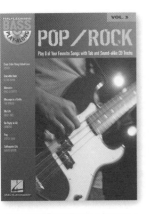

The Bass Play-Along™ Series will help you play your favorite songs quickly and easily! Just follow the tab, listen to the CD to hear how the bass should sound, and then play along using the separate backing tracks. The melody and lyrics are also included in the book in case you want to sing, or to simply help you follow along. The CD is enhanced so you can use your computer to adjust the recording to any tempo without changing pitch!

1. Rock
00699674 Book/CD Pack $12.95

2. R&B
00699675 Book/CD Pack $12.95

3. Pop/Rock
00699677 Book/CD Pack $12.95

4. '90s Rock
00699679 Book/CD Pack $12.95

5. Funk
00699680 Book/CD Pack $12.95

6. Classic Rock
00699678 Book/CD Pack $12.95

7. Hard Rock
00699676 Book/CD Pack $14.95

8. Punk Rock
00699813 Book/CD Pack $12.95

9. Blues
00699817 Book/CD Pack $12.95

10. Jimi Hendrix Smash Hits
00699815 Book/CD Pack $16.95

11. Country
00699818 Book/CD Pack $12.95

12. Punk Classics
00699814 Book/CD Pack $12.99

13. Lennon & McCartney
00699816 Book/CD Pack $14.99

14. Modern Rock
00699821 Book/CD Pack $14.99

15. Mainstream Rock
00699822 Book/CD Pack $14.99

16. '80s Metal
00699825 Book/CD Pack $16.99

17. Pop Metal
00699826 Book/CD Pack $14.99

18. Blues Rock
00699828 Book/CD Pack $14.99

19. Steely Dan
00700203 Book/CD Pack $16.99

20. The Police
00700270 Book/CD Pack $14.99

21. Rock Band – Modern Rock
00700705 Book/CD Pack $14.95

22. Rock Band – Classic Rock
00700706 Book/CD Pack $14.95

**23. Pink Floyd –
Dark Side of The Moon**
00700847 Book/CD Pack $14.99

24. Weezer
00700960 Book/CD Pack $14.99

25. Nirvana
00701047 Book/CD Pack $14.99

26. Black Sabbath
00701180 Book/CD Pack $14.99

27. Kiss
00701181 Book/CD Pack $14.99

31. The 1970s
00701185 Book/CD Pack $14.99

33. Christmas Hits
00701197 Book/CD Pack $12.99

34. Easy Songs
00701480 Book/CD Pack $12.99

FOR MORE INFORMATION,
SEE YOUR LOCAL MUSIC DEALER,
OR WRITE TO:

HAL•LEONARD®
CORPORATION
7777 W. BLUEMOUND RD. P.O. BOX 13819
MILWAUKEE, WISCONSIN 53213

Visit Hal Leonard Online at **www.halleonard.com**

Prices, contents, and availability
subject to change without notice.

1010

BASS RECORDED VERSIONS

Bass Recorded Versions feature authentic transcriptions written in standard notation and tablature for bass guitar. This series features complete bass lines from the classics to contemporary superstars.

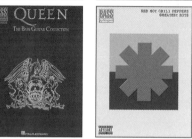
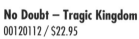

25 All-Time Rock Bass Classics
00690445 / $14.95

25 Essential Rock Bass Classics
00690210 / $15.95

Aerosmith Bass Collection
00690413 / $17.95

Best of Victor Bailey
00690718 / $19.95

Bass Tab 1990-1999
00690400 / $16.95

Bass Tab 1999-2000
00690404 / $14.95

Bass Tab White Pages
00690508 / $29.99

The Beatles Bass Lines
00690170 / $14.95

The Beatles 1962-1966
00690556 / $18.99

The Beatles 1967-1970
00690557 / $19.99

Best Bass Rock Hits
00694803 / $12.95

**Black Sabbath –
We Sold Our Soul for Rock 'N' Roll**
00660116 / $17.95

The Best of Blink 182
00690549 / $18.95

Blues Bass Classics
00690291 / $14.95

Boston Bass Collection
00690935 / $19.95

Chart Hits for Bass
00690729 / $14.95

The Best of Eric Clapton
00660187 / $19.95

Stanley Clarke Collection
00672307 / $19.95

Funk Bass Bible
00690744 / $19.95

Hard Rock Bass Bible
00690746 / $17.95

**Jimi Hendrix –
Are You Experienced?**
00690371 / $17.95

The Buddy Holly Bass Book
00660132 / $12.95

Incubus – Morning View
00690639 / $17.95

Iron Maiden Bass Anthology
00690867 / $22.99

Best of Kiss for Bass
00690080 / $19.95

**Lynyrd Skynyrd –
All-Time Greatest Hits**
00690956 / $19.99

Bob Marley Bass Collection
00690568 / $19.95

Mastodon – Crack the Skye
00691007 / $19.99

Best of Marcus Miller
00690811 / $22.99

Motown Bass Classics
00690253 / $14.95

Mudvayne – Lost & Found
00690798 / $19.95

Nirvana Bass Collection
00690066 / $19.95

No Doubt – Tragic Kingdom
00120112 / $22.95

The Offspring – Greatest Hits
00690809 / $17.95

**Jaco Pastorius –
Greatest Jazz Fusion Bass Player**
00690421 / $17.95

The Essential Jaco Pastorius
00690420 / $19.99

Pearl Jam – Ten
00694882 / $14.95

Pink Floyd – Dark Side of the Moon
00660172 / $14.95

The Best of Police
00660207 / $14.95

Pop/Rock Bass Bible
00690747 / $17.95

Queen – The Bass Collection
00690065 / $17.95

R&B Bass Bible
00690745 / $17.95

Rage Against the Machine
00690248 / $17.99

The Best of Red Hot Chili Peppers
00695285 / $24.95

**Red Hot Chili Peppers –
Blood Sugar Sex Magik**
00690064 / $19.95

Red Hot Chili Peppers – By the Way
00690585 / $19.95

**Red Hot Chili Peppers –
Californication**
00690390 / $19.95

**Red Hot Chili Peppers –
Greatest Hits**
00690675 / $18.95

**Red Hot Chili Peppers –
One Hot Minute**
00690091 / $18.95

**Red Hot Chili Peppers –
Stadium Arcadium**
00690853 / $24.95

**Red Hot Chili Peppers –
Stadium Arcadium: Deluxe Edition**
Book/2-CD Pack
00690863 / $39.95

Rock Bass Bible
00690446 / $19.95

Rolling Stones
00690256 / $16.95

Top Hits for Bass
00690677 / $14.95

**Stevie Ray Vaughan –
Lightnin' Blues 1983-1987**
00694778 / $19.95

1010